Artificial Intelligence
Thinking Like a Human

Julie Ellis

Artificial Intelligence: Thinking Like a Human

Text: Julie Ellis
Publishers: Tania Mazzeo and Eliza Webb
Series consultant: Amanda Sutera
Hands on Heads Consulting
Editor: Kirstie Innes-Will
Project editor: Annabel Smith
Designer: Leigh Ashforth
Project designer: Danielle Maccarone
Permissions researchers: Lumina Datamatics
Production controller: Renee Tome

Acknowledgements
We would like to thank the following for permission to reproduce copyright material:

Front cover: Vladislav Ociacia/Adobe Stock Photos; p. 4: garo002/Shutterstock.com; p.5: metamorworks/Shutterstock.com; p. 6: Gorodenkoff/Shutterstock.com; p. 7 (title page): PeopleImages.com - Yuri A/Shutterstock.com; p. 8, back cover: Thapana_Studio/Shutterstock.com; p. 9: (top) Patryk Kosmider/Shutterstock.com; (bottom) Ground Picture/Shutterstock.com; p. 10: Poznyakov/Shutterstock.com; p. 11: iStock.com/travelism; pp. 12, 13: atDigit/Alamy Stock Photo; p. 14: JYPIX/Alamy Stock Photo; p. 15: Hollie Adams/Getty Images News/Getty Images; p. 16: JEAN-CHRISTOPHE VERHAEGEN/AFP/Getty Images; p. 17: VCG/Visual China Group/Getty Images; p. 18: China News Service/China News Service/Getty Images; p. 19: (top) iStock.com/PaulGulea; (bottom) iStock.com/sumnersgraphicsinc; p. 20: EarlyBird/Alamy Stock Photo; p. 21: iStock.com/valio84sl; p. 22: A_Lesik/Shutterstock.com; p. 23: Andrey Moisseyev/Alamy Stock Photo; p. 24: Simon/Adobe Stock Photos; p. 25: Kilito Chan/Moment/Getty Images; p.26: vectorfusionart/Adobe Stock Photos; p. 27: Prapat Aowsakorn/Shutterstock.com; p. 28: iStock.com/Inside Creative House; p. 29: Danko/Adobe Stock Photos; p. 30: Krzysztof Jakubczyk/Alamy Stock Photo.

Every effort has been made to trace and acknowledge copyright. However, if any infringement has occurred, the publishers tender their apologies and invite the copyright holders to contact them.

NovaStar

ISBN 978 0 17 033516 4

Cengage Learning Australia
Level 5, 80 Dorcas Street
Southbank VIC 3006 Australia
Phone: 1300 790 853
Email: aust.nelsonprimary@cengage.com

For learning solutions, visit **cengage.com.au**

Printed in China by 1010 Printing International Ltd
1 2 3 4 5 6 7 29 28 27 26 25

Nelson acknowledges the Traditional Owners and Custodians of the lands of all First Nations Peoples. We pay respect to Elders past and present, and extend that respect to all First Nations Peoples today.

Contents

What Is Artificial Intelligence (AI)?	**4**
Different Kinds of AI	**6**
AI in Everyday Life	**8**
Understanding How AI Works	**12**
AI Robots	**16**
The Benefits of AI	**20**
The Risks of AI	**22**
Using AI Safely	**24**
Future Planning for AI	**26**
Is AI Harmful or Helpful?	**28**
The Future Is in Our Hands	**30**
Glossary	**31**
Index	**32**

What Is Artificial Intelligence (AI)?

Artificial Intelligence (AI) is a computer's ability to think and learn like a human. AI computer systems mimic how humans solve problems or perform tasks. All AI has something in common: the ability to improve over time through "learning" experiences.

AI works by **analysing** huge amounts of **data** very quickly and noticing patterns. AI can do work that is dull, dangerous, dirty, or difficult for humans, such as analysing lots of data quickly.

AI is a complex technology, but it is not human. It is just a tool. So what can it do?

BIG DATA

AI needs so much data to generate new material that this data is called "big data".

Find Patterns

Some computer systems are taught to find hidden patterns in large amounts of data and make decisions without human help. An app can find patterns in the songs someone likes and can recommend new songs with similar patterns. This is called **machine learning**.

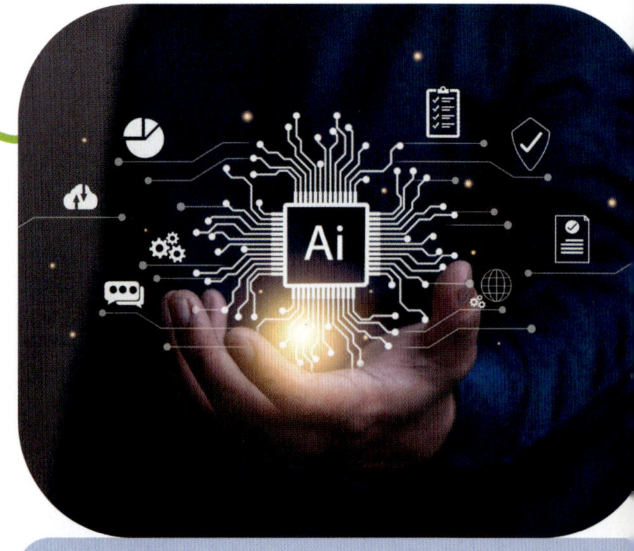

AI is used in many aspects of everyday life.

Answer Questions

Voice-activated software uses AI to listen for key words when you talk to it, and then answers your question or carries out your instruction.

See Like a Human

A self-driving car has **sensors** that work like human eyes to identify different parts of an image. The car will stop when its sensors see a red traffic light, because the sensors have been trained to recognise and stop at that image.

This driverless car uses sensors to move through traffic safely.

Different Kinds of AI

Computer scientists refer to the type of AI in use today as artificial narrow intelligence (ANI). It's called "narrow" because it needs to be programmed by humans. Different categories of ANI have different abilities.

Reactive ANI reacts to situations based on preprogrammed rules. It can react quickly, but it cannot learn or adapt. A chess program can use preprogrammed rules to analyse the chess board and then make moves against a human **opponent**.

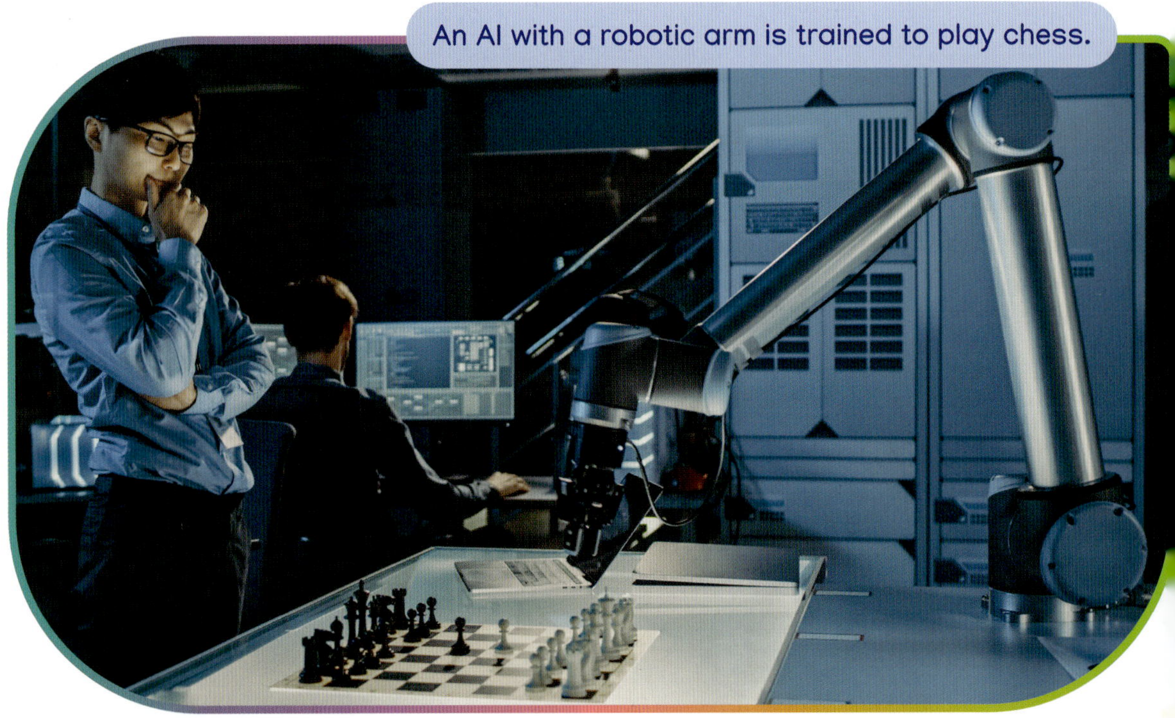

An AI with a robotic arm is trained to play chess.

Limited memory ANI can use past experiences to learn and adapt its responses, but its memory is limited. AlphaGo is a computer program that plays a board game, using past games to help it make new decisions. Because AlphaGo's memory is limited, it can only learn from games in its recent past.

Unlimited memory ANI also uses past experiences to learn and adapt its responses. Because it has unlimited memory, it can link old data with current data to make new data. This is called deep learning (DL). Software with **image recognition** uses unlimited memory.

Image recognition can be used to keep your electronic information safe.

FUTURE AI?

Experts have named two more types of AI, but they don't exist yet.

Artificial general intelligence (AGI) would be equal to humans in intelligence.

Artificial super intelligence (ASI) would be superior to humans.

AI in Everyday Life

There are many ways AI technology makes our everyday lives easier and more enjoyable. It can perform boring tasks, act as a memory prompt, help us learn and help keep us healthy and entertained.

Boring Tasks

AI-powered personal assistants can answer questions, set reminders, control smart devices, manage schedules and even order groceries.

Memory Prompts

Shopping websites with AI use machine learning to recommend products based on what a person has looked at or bought previously. AI-powered **chatbots** can answer your questions about items for sale in **real time**. This makes shopping quicker and sometimes more fun.

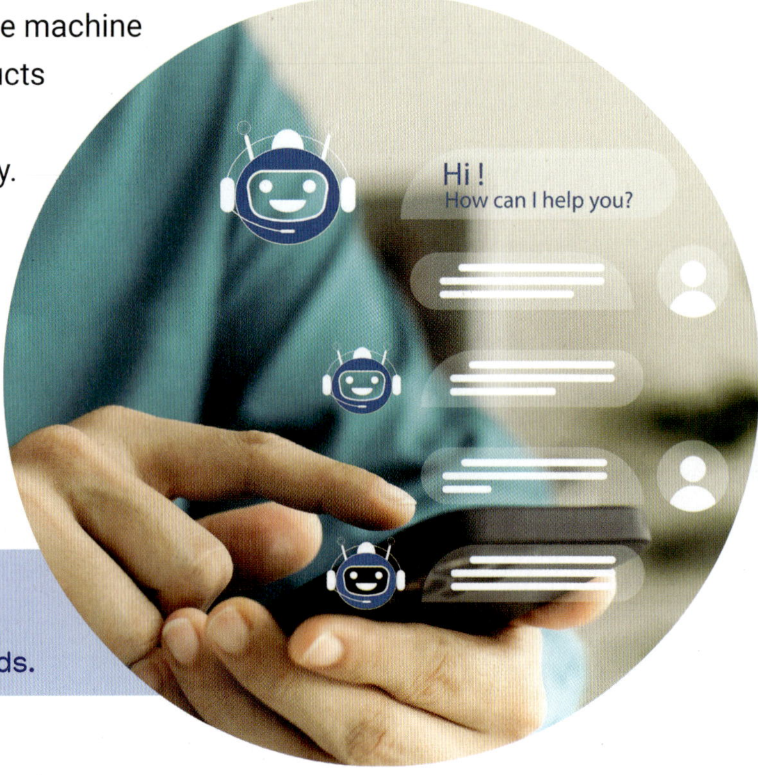

Online stores often have chatbots that give advice on the best product for your needs.

AI FOR NAVIGATION

In map apps in vehicles and on phones, AI analyses traffic data, such as roadworks and accidents. It then shows drivers the quickest route to their destination.

Help Us Learn

In most schools, teachers use devices such as tablets and laptops to deliver lessons. AI-powered **search engines**, chatbots and apps can provide students with instant feedback, immediate information on any topic and **personalised** learning, helping them to learn faster and more easily.

These children are using computers to help them learn how to program robots.

Keep Us Healthy

Smartwatches that use AI can tell the wearer about their health and fitness levels. AI can analyse health data to identify patterns and risks, and provide personalised recommendations for diet and exercise. This provides people with information to make good decisions about their individual health and lifestyle.

Children can use special smartwatches to keep in touch with friends and family safely.

Entertain Us

In video games, AI is used to make characters that aren't controlled by another player respond intelligently, in human-like ways. This can make video games more exciting, because AI creates smarter opponents that can adapt to your playing ability.

AI can make video games more exciting.

In online platforms, AI can suggest movies and TV shows that a person might like, based on what they have previously watched.

Understanding How AI Works

AI works by mimicking the way a human brain works. For example, using image recognition technology, AI learns to recognise what a cat is by seeing many different cats in many different **digital** images, in the same way you learnt to recognise what a cat is by seeing different cats over time. The AI program is not told what "makes" a cat. It must recognise patterns in data over time and learn on its own.

The AI is trained using data (pictures of cats). The more pictures of cats it is shown, the better it becomes at recognising "cat". It can be shown cats in shadow or light, cats from the front, back or side, sitting, standing, running or jumping.

Every time the AI identifies a new cat, that information is added to its memory to improve the AI's cat-recognition skills.

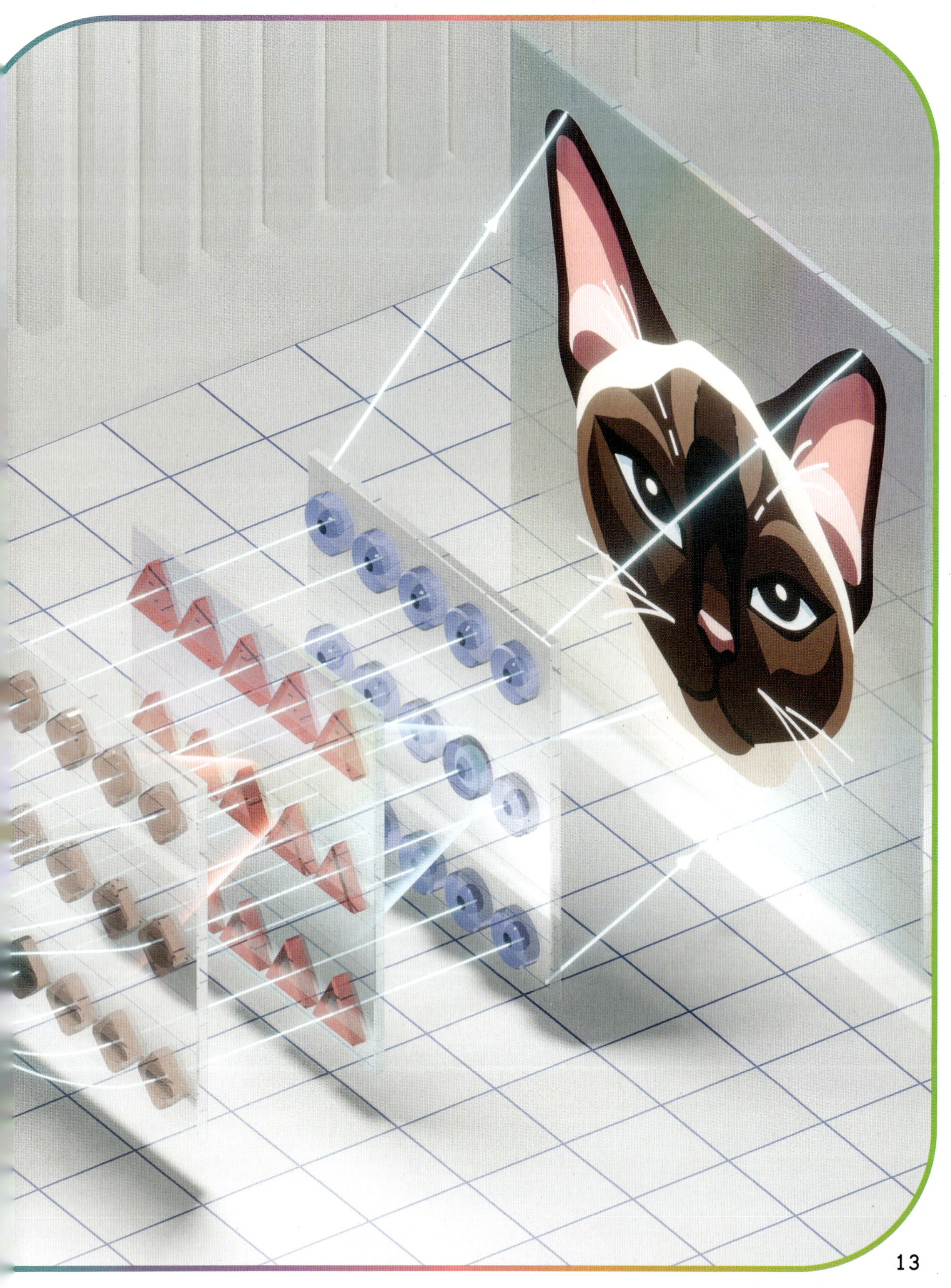

Generative Learning

Generative learning is when AI takes data and creates, or generates, new information that has not existed before.

The AI program ChatGPT trains itself by reading a large amount of text. It looks for patterns in the text and makes a set of rules to help it predict the next words. This type of AI is called a large language model. When someone asks ChatGPT to produce some text (based on guidelines they provide), the AI follows the patterns and rules to generate new text.

The AI program ChatGPT can be trained to produce text for users.

Making New Artworks

When a generative AI system is given a lot of examples of someone's work, it can use machine learning to create a new work that is similar. Many writers, artists and composers are worried that their unique creations might be given to an AI system without their consent or knowledge. They are concerned they will not get paid for the text, images or songs that AI produces based on their creativity.

Generative AI is a risk to Indigenous art, because Indigenous art connects to the past, and to culture and Country. It cannot be created by non-Indigenous people or by AI.

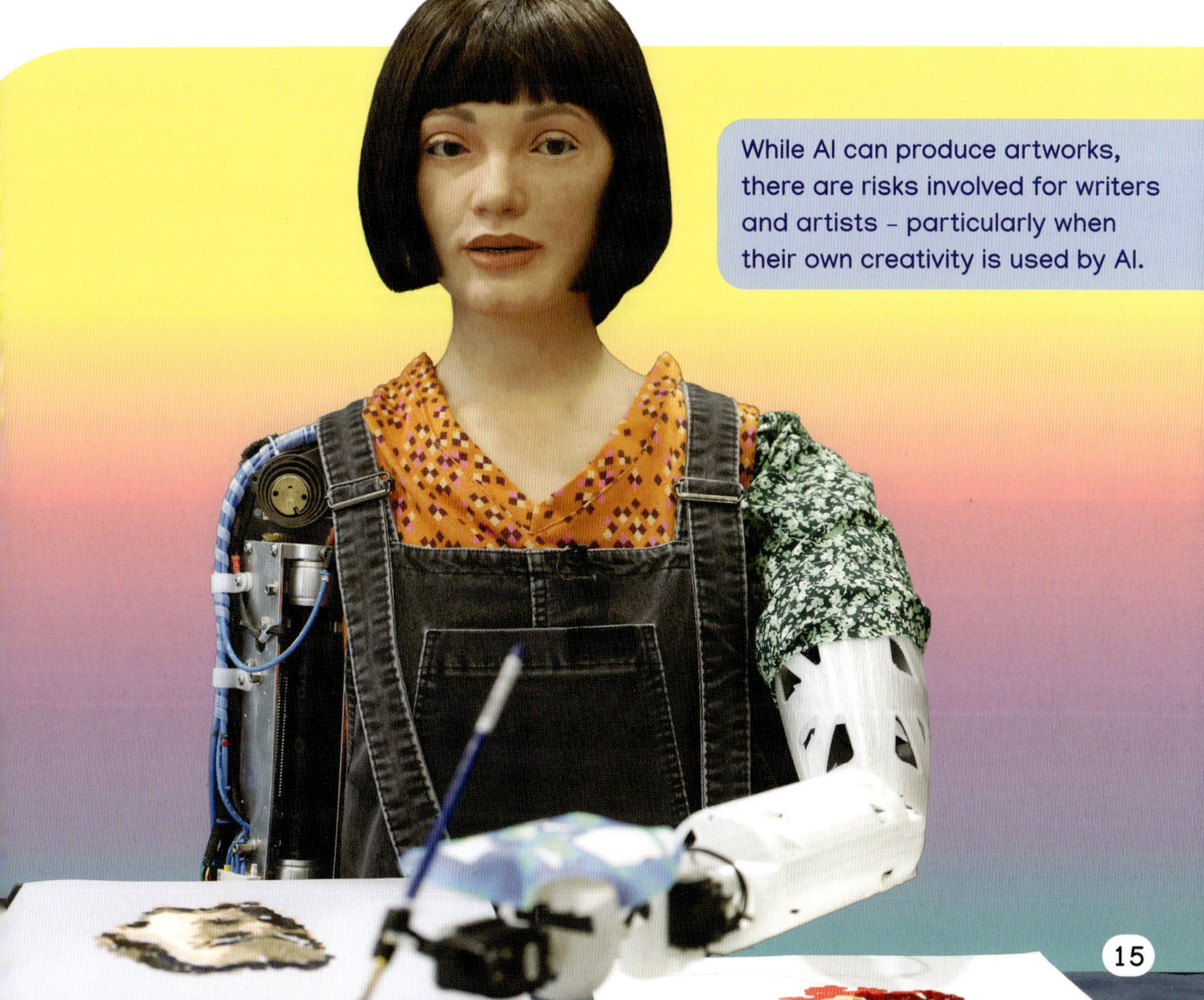

While AI can produce artworks, there are risks involved for writers and artists – particularly when their own creativity is used by AI.

AI Robots

Not all robots have AI. Robots without AI do repetitive tasks and are known as autonomous robots. Autonomous robots can wash planes, weld and even help with medical surgery.

Robots with AI can change their behaviour based on **sensory feedback**. They can do some jobs better than people, because they:

- can make decisions faster
- can see in the dark and can move underwater
- don't get distracted by stress in dangerous situations
- can learn quickly from experience and immediately improve their performance
- can do repetitive or complicated tasks without getting tired.

KINDS OF ROBOTS

AI robots can be either humanoid or non-humanoid.

This headless dog-sized robot has been designed to scare wildlife away from an airport in Alaska, USA.

Humanoid Robots

Humanoid robots have a human shape. They are used in many different settings, including the entertainment and service industries, the military, and social and education settings. Humanoid robots are a useful AI tool. They fill a gap between humans and machines.

One type of humanoid robot, called a social robot, is designed to interact with people and keep them company. Social robots can learn from their experiences to talk with humans.

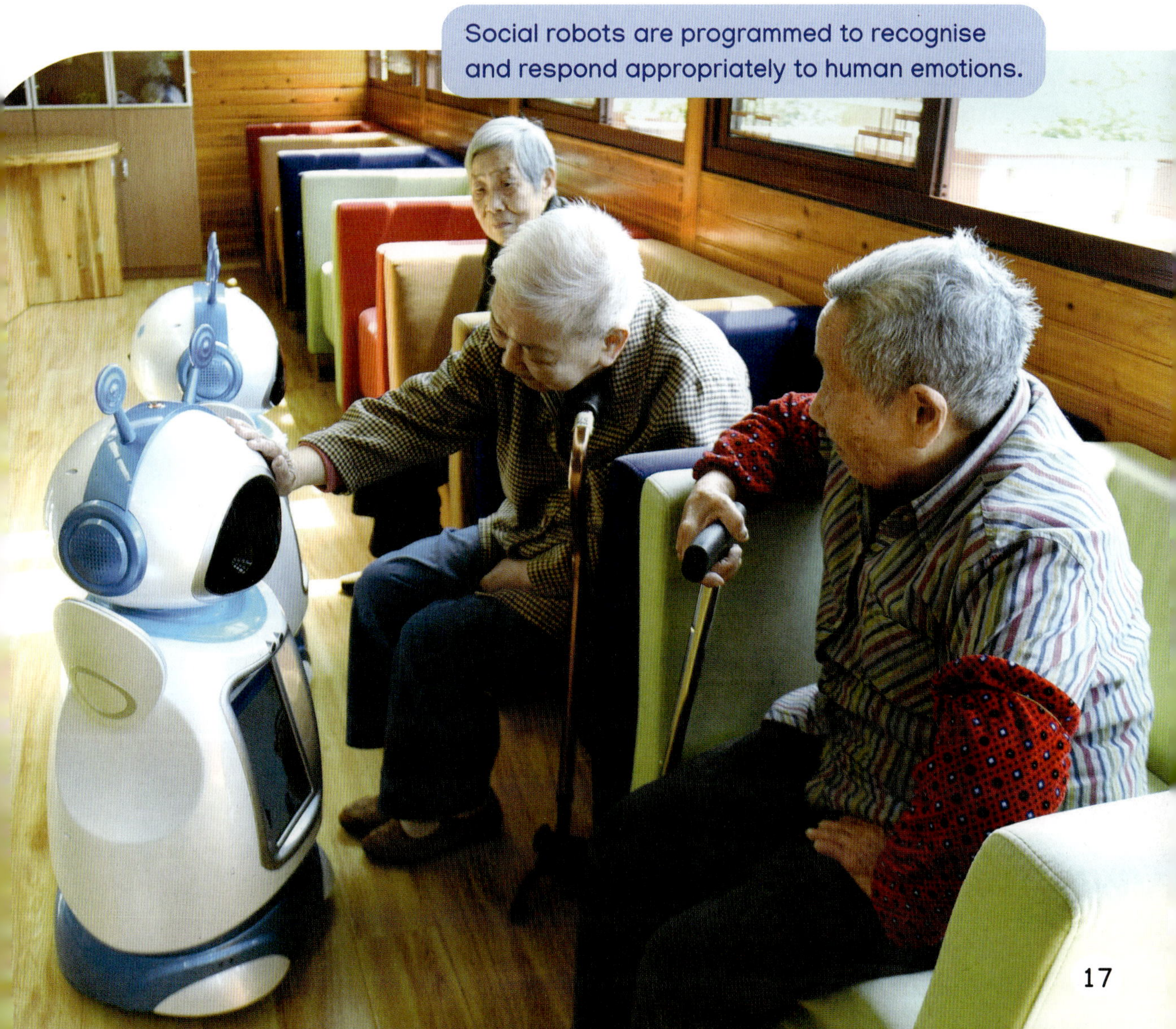

Social robots are programmed to recognise and respond appropriately to human emotions.

Non-Humanoid Robots

Sometimes it works better if the AI robot does not have a human shape. For example, AI robots with wheels are used to explore the rough surface of Mars. Non-humanoid robots do work that is dull, dirty, difficult or dangerous.

DULL

In warehouses, AI robots can move down long aisles, find items, scan them and transport them to the packing area. Robots can work without a break and make fewer mistakes than humans, so they save the business money.

DIRTY

A robot with AI can inspect, monitor and clean a tunnel or pipe before problems arise.

Robots can be used in spaces that are difficult to access or for dirty, uncomfortable work.

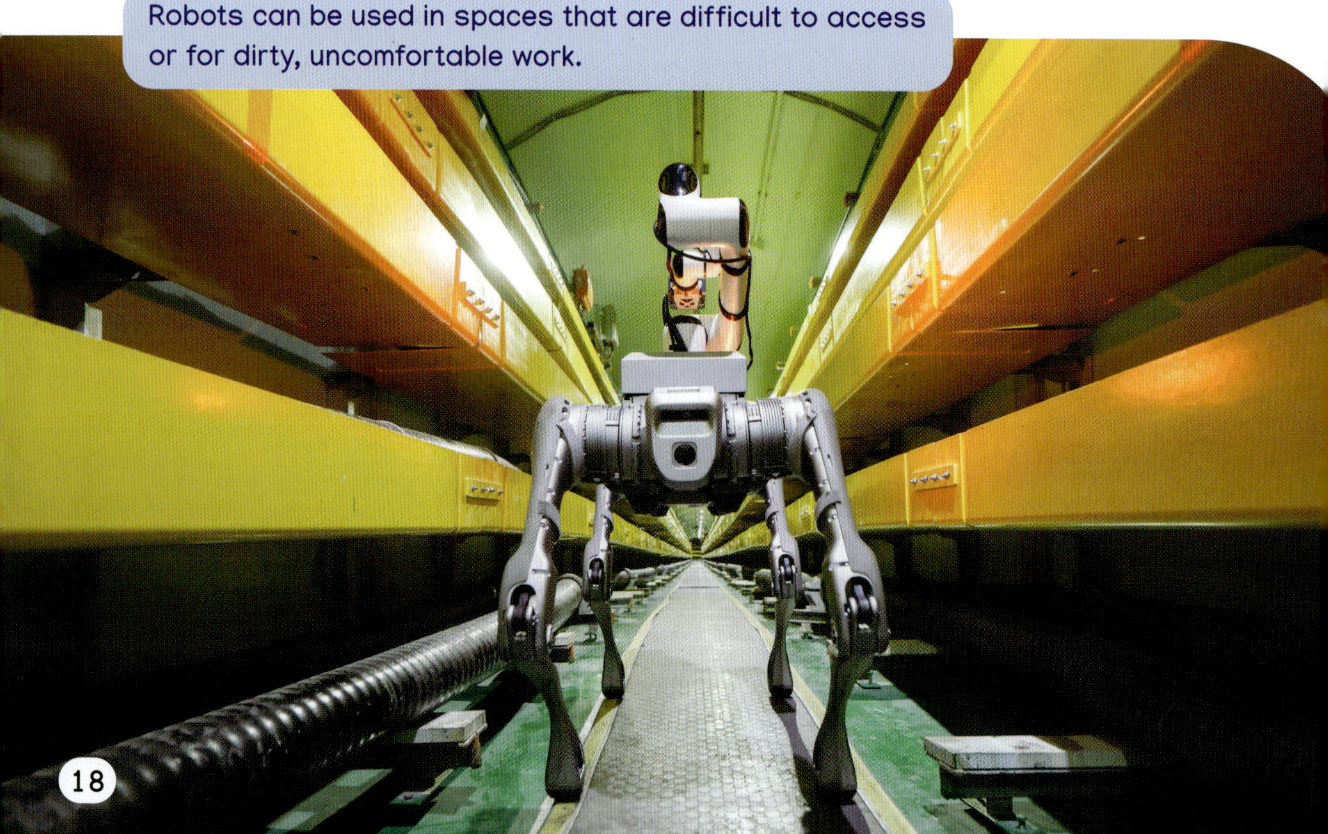

DANGEROUS

An AI rescue robot can fit into small spaces, such as under a collapsed building after an earthquake, where it's not safe for a person to crawl. It can use cameras and other sensors to look for human survivors.

This robot helps with the dangerous and difficult work of fire-fighting.

DIFFICULT

Sydney Harbour Bridge has climbing AI robots that can scan, map and clean the bridge without human help.

Looking after Sydney Harbour Bridge is complex, so having robots who can do a lot of the work is very helpful.

The Benefits of AI

Artificial intelligence can be combined with Indigenous Knowledge, to help Traditional Owners solve challenges and threats in their environments.

AI and Indigenous Knowledge Help Magpie Geese Return to the Wetlands

The Bininj people have hunted magpie geese for food in the Narab wetlands in Kakadu National Park , Northern Territory, for about 65 000 years. But when a weed called para grass began choking the wetlands, the magpie geese stopped nesting there.

Thousands of magpie geese nested in the Narab wetlands every year, until a weed threatened their habitat.

The para grass overpowered plants that the geese liked to eat. There was no food for the geese and their chicks, and no space for the geese to build their nests of floating reeds.

In 2019, Kakadu rangers began using **drones** to monitor where para grass is growing, and how many magpie geese there are. The drones take photos, then AI software uses image recognition to identify magpie geese, para grass and native plants.
The rangers then make informed decisions about where to spray or burn para grass. By reducing the para grass, the rangers are encouraging the geese to return to the wetlands.

Rangers learnt to guide drones to monitor the para grass.

The Risks of AI

Because AI is not human, it does not have the emotions, creativity or ethical awareness that humans have. AI can make mistakes if the data it is given has errors in it. It can also be used for bad purposes.

- AI can be **biased** because it only learns from the information it is given. If a system is given information that refers to all doctors as "he" and all nurses as "she", it will conclude that doctors are male and nurses are female and will base future decisions on this incorrect information.
- AI can **plagiarise** or even create **deepfakes**, which show a person saying or doing things they never actually said or did.
- AI can "hallucinate", or see patterns that don't exist. This happens when it combines information from different data sets and makes an incorrect conclusion.
- AI could be used in weapons. What if some countries start using robots as weapons?

We may need new laws to make sure that AI drones are not used to hurt people or invade their privacy.

If we rely on AI to run driverless vehicles, what happens if they break down or make a mistake?

- AI can be bad for the environment. Generative AI requires an enormous amount of power to generate calculations, and lots of fresh water to keep the computers cool.
- AI can collect large amounts of personal data, which could be misused. AI can also be used in hacking.
- AI might take the place of human relationships. Because some AI robots look lifelike, people might bond more with a robot companion than with people in real life.

Using AI Safely

AI is a very useful tool for humans, but we have to be careful when using it. Society must create guidelines to ensure AI is used **ethically** and responsibly.

Here are some ways we can use AI-powered computer systems safely:

1. Remember, AI isn't human. It can make mistakes. A chatbot can sound like a human, but it isn't real.

2. You are responsible for checking how accurate the information AI gives you is. Ask it for source links and check the links.

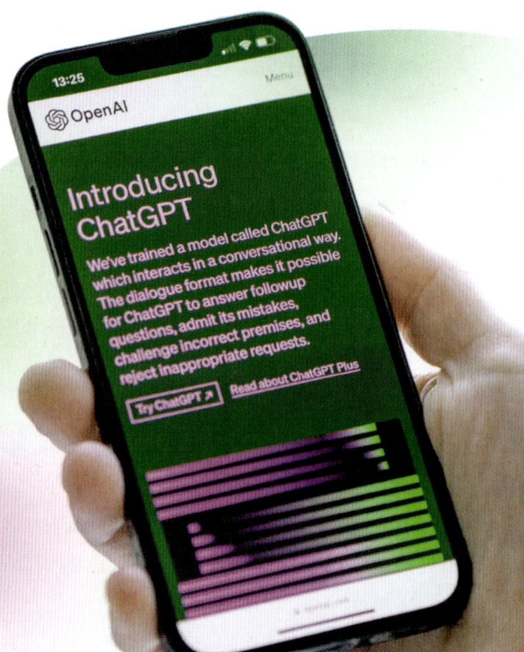

Large language models of AI can do amazing things, but they also provide incorrect information sometimes.

3. Control where AI leads you. If AI is generating content you don't want, rephrase your questions and keep to your main topic.

4. If one AI isn't working for you, try a different one.

5. Ask for more. If the AI answer is unexpected or unclear, ask for more information.

It's important to be cautious when using anything generated by AI.

Future Planning for AI

Imagine a world where AI machines do most of the work and humans have more free time and resources. If humans want the benefits of AI, we need to plan for our future with this tool.

Changing Jobs

If AI takes over most of the jobs traditionally done by humans, humans will work fewer hours or do jobs that have not yet been invented.

Data Protection

AI can be used to hack or steal data from companies or organisations, so it is important that countries have laws that protect the data stored in that country.

Hacking has become a major problem worldwide.

Rules

Governments need to agree how countries will use AI ethically, for example, not using AI in certain situations in war.

Equal Access

We need to consider how we will make sure everyone has equal access to AI so they can benefit from it, including people who have less money or live in isolated areas.

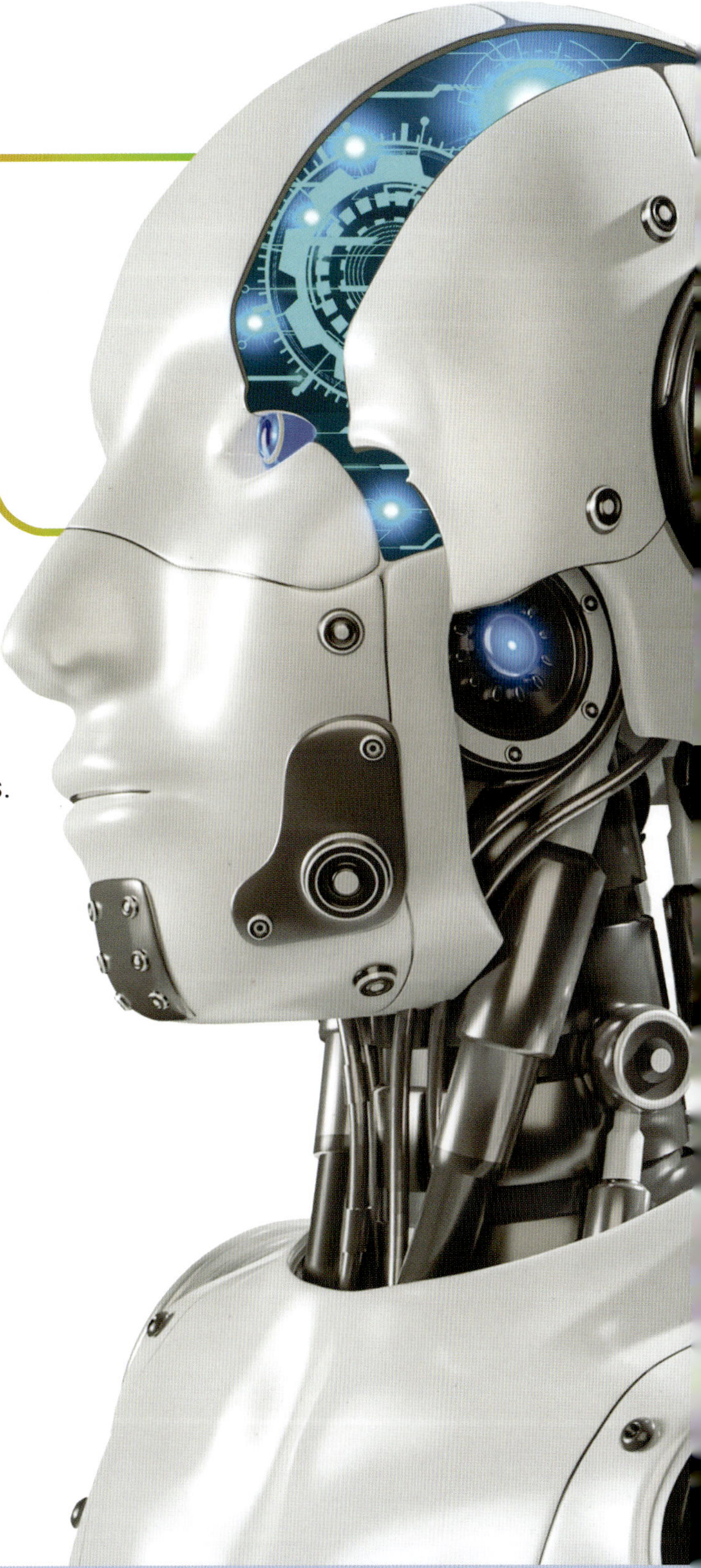

THINK ABOUT ...

Is it fair if humans are not paid for new works based on their creativity?

Will generative AI mean that we no longer need human writers, artists and composers?

Wealthier countries currently have an advantage in being able to develop AI and robots.

Is AI Harmful or Helpful?

The Grade 6 students at Green Bay Primary School are discussing whether AI is a great invention or not. They have to write an exposition explaining their opinion.

I think artificial intelligence is great! AI helps us do things faster and better. Have you ever used a voice assistant to set a timer or find out the weather? That's AI at work!

AI can also help solve big problems, like finding cures for diseases or predicting natural disasters. Scientists use AI to analyse data and come up with solutions to all kinds of challenges.

AI can learn and improve over time. Just like how you get better at a game the more you play it, AI can get smarter as it learns from new information. So I think AI is very helpful for humans.

Kirra

I think we should be worried about artificial intelligence. In the movies, sometimes the robots turn against humans. AI could become dangerous if we're not careful.

Another worry is that since robots can do things better and faster than humans, companies are starting to use robots instead of people. How will people get money if they lose their jobs?

Also, AI can be wrong sometimes. If the data AI is given is biased, the AI might make unfair decisions.

Finally, AI can collect tons of data about us, like what we buy online or where we go. If this data gets into the wrong hands, it could be used against us—or used to create deepfakes.

AI is definitely useful, but we need to be careful in how we use it.

Oliver

The Future Is in Our Hands

AI is a tool that has the power to transform our lives, but only if we use it responsibly. Governments need to create rules so that everyone has fair access to AI and it is used safely. And we all need to be careful that we use it ethically.

In 2016, British scientist Stephen Hawking said:

"The rise of powerful AI will either be the best or the worst thing ever to happen to humanity. We do not yet know which."

Many scientists agree with Stephen Hawking that we need to be very careful in how we use AI.

What do you think the world will look like with more AI?

Glossary

analysing (*verb*)	studying closely, examining and explaining
biased (*adjective*)	unfair, based on information that is incomplete or not correct
chatbots (*noun*)	computer programs that conduct a conversation, either in type or using an artificial voice
data (*noun*)	a collection of information, such as images, audio or text
deepfakes (*noun*)	images that have been manipulated to put one person's features on someone else
digital (*adjective*)	storing, using or sending information electronically
drones (*noun*)	remote-controlled flying objects
ethically (*adverb*)	in a manner that is in line with what is fair or right
image recognition (*noun*)	the ability of computers to identify and classify specific things within digital images and videos
machine learning (*noun*)	where machines use large amounts of data to make decisions
opponent (*noun*)	the person you play a game against
personalised (*adjective*)	made to suit the needs and preferences of a particular person
plagiarise (*verb*)	to copy from other sources without acknowledging the original creator or paying them
real time (*noun*)	the same time that information is received
search engines (*noun*)	websites that allow people to look up information on the internet
sensors (*noun*)	machines that can sense and collect information about movement, light and other things
sensory feedback (*noun*)	feedback from the senses, such as touch, hearing, sight or sound
voice-activated software (*noun*)	a computer program that responds to human voices

Index

AlphaGo 6
analysis 4, 6, 9, 10, 28, 31
apps 4, 9
artificial general intelligence (AGI) 7
artificial narrow intelligence (ANI) 6–7
artificial super intelligence (ASI) 7
artwork 14–15
autonomous robots 16
bias 22, 29, 31
Bininj people 20–21
board games 6
chatbots 8, 9, 24, 31
ChatGPT 14
creativity 15, 27
data 4, 7, 9, 10, 12, 14, 22, 23, 26, 28, 29, 31
data protection 26
deep learning (DL) 7
deepfakes 22, 28, 31
digital images 12–13, 14–15
driverless vehicles 5, 23
drones 21, 22, 31
equal access 27
ethics 24–25, 30, 31
fire-fighting robot 19
future planning 26–27
generative learning 14, 23, 24, 27
governments 27, 30
hacking 23, 26
Hawking, Stephen 30
health 8, 10
humanoid robots 16, 17, 23
image recognition 7, 12, 23, 31
Indigenous art 15
Indigenous Knowledge 20–21
jobs 26, 28
Kakadu National Park 20–21
large language models 1, 14, 24
laws 22, 26
limited memory ANI 6, 7
machine learning 4, 8, 15, 31
magpie geese 22–23
memory prompts 8
navigation 9
non-humanoid robots 16, 18
opponents 6, 11, 31
personal assistants 8
plagiarism 22, 31
privacy 22
reactive ANI 6
real time 8, 31
robots 16–19, 22, 23, 27, 29
safety 5, 7, 10, 19, 24–25, 30
scientists 6, 28, 30
search engines 9, 31
self-driving vehicles 5, 23
sensors 5, 31
sensory feedback 16, 31
shopping 8
smartwatches 10
social robots 17
surgery 16
Sydney Harbour Bridge 19
unlimited memory ANI 7
video games 11
voice-activated software 5, 31
weapons 22